T0198564

POETRY
FROM THE
CABIN PORCH

DANNY MAHLON UNDERWOOD

AuthorHouse™
1663 Liberty Drive
Bloomington, IN 47403
www.authorhouse.com
Phone: 1 (800) 839-8640

This book is printed on acid-free paper.

ISBN: 978-1-7283-4801-8 (sc)
ISBN: 978-1-7283-4802-5 (e)

Print information available on the last page.

Published by AuthorHouse 02/24/2020

CONTENTS

'POETRY FROM THE CABIN PORCH' is all about the outdoors, hunting & cabin life down at my farm in Southern Illinois.

The farm has not only provided me with a hunting spot for the last 14 years, but has also provided a writing sanctuary for me and a relaxing place for friends and family to unwind from the daily grind.

Every one of the 24 poems in this book, were written either in the cabin or while sitting on the porch of the cabin.

JUNE 16, 2018

Give me a dirt road;
Surrounded by trees.
Splashes of sunshine;
A gentle breeze.

A cooking fire;
A handful of close friends.
A relaxing day;
That I hope never ends.

The flag flying proud;
From the porch rail.
Memories to make;
Stories to tell.

At the end of the day;
Let us give praise.
With our heads bowed;
And glasses raised.

OAKTREE BALLET

As I sit in this tree;
Listening to the rain of the dead.
Not of chaotic mayhem or destruction;
The scenes take away your breath.

The brittle brown leaves;
Pushed to earth by layers of snow.
Alerted by snapping sounds;
That proceed the elegant show.

Drifting and twirling in mid air;
Like a dancer leaping across the stage.
Landing ever so gently;
As the circle of life turns the page.

A bare tree stands silent;
As though it is in mourning.
The lady will stay dressed in black;
Until she blooms again next Spring.

BINGE WATCHING

Some folks like viewing Downton Abbey;
Or every episode of the S.O.A.
A marathon of classic horror films;
The Walking Dead fills their every day.

Me, I'm not much into T.V. shows;
Or hours on the couch sitting around.
But tonight I'm glued to this bar stool;
Binge watching beers go down.

Once in awhile I'll mix it up;
Like the commercials and ad spots.
Instead of sipping on the frosty mug;
I'll throw down a vodka shot.

I hope my show never gets cancelled;
It's a great cast and crew.
There is a few cameos by Smirnoff;
And it stars my favorite brew.

So keep your series and soaps;
Sharkweek, sports and Cougar Town.
Tonight I'm glued to this bar stool;
Binge watching these beers go down.

GAMING COUNTRY STYLE

The sun has given way to clouds;
Light sprinkles are falling down.
I'm staring out the cabin door;
Watching the guineas run around.

They are playing in the rain;
Like we used to do as kids.
Squawking and flapping their wings;
As if they're playing tag and saying, "You're It".

Nature is taking place everyday;
Although most people don't get to see it.
Here comes one of the oil workers;
Making sure the pump doesn't quit.

Who knew a mostly vacant farm;
Would have so much activity going on.
But these things are happening every day;
Even the times when I'm gone.

Man I thought I had a good life;
However, what I been doing ain't livin'.
Livin' is playing in the rain;
Like the carefree cousins of the chicken.

So I put on my rubber boots;
And headed out into the rain.
I wonder if the guineas;
Will let me join their game.

FARMFIELDS AND FEATHERS

The humidity has dropped like the temperature;
The beans have turned to thin sticks.
The corn is now brown and brittle;
Instead of lush, green and thick.

The clouds are floating cotton balls;
Against a beautiful field of blue.
The calendar about to turn to fall;
Summer is all but through.

The air is cool and crisp;
Requires a jacket to start the day.
A gentle twist of the throttle;
And I am on my way.

A ride through the country side;
Surrounded by nothing but farm fields.
A turkey buzzard bursts from the ditch;
Flying just feet in front of my windshield.

Not a normal encounter during a bike ride;
A tale not frequently heard.
But it isn't the first time I was buzzed;
And subsequently got flipped the bird.

FROST AND THE FULL MOOM

An hour before legal shooting time;
I stumble out the cabin door.
As the cold air blasts my face;
I wonder what I do this for.

By chance I may see a deer;
Or slimmer odds I may get a shot.
If you know anything about probabilities;
With the averages of bow hunting, probably not.

But I'll bet against the odds;
For a chance at God provided meat.
I'm not concerned or obsessed with antlers;
And I only kill as much as I will eat.

But what drives me into the woods;
And to get me out of bed this soon.
Is to spend time alone with God;
Energized by the frost and full moon.

There is no greater joy in life;
Than to get one on one with my God.
And once in a while he takes pity;
He even lets me beat the odds.

RAINDROPS AND WRITING

Raindrops can delay baseball games;
Keep farm equipment in the shed.
Ruin your backyard cookouts;
Keep the most dedicated hunter in bed.

It can make you run for cover;
With all the thunder and lightning.
But nothing better than a downpour;
To entice a poet to get to writing.

Something about the rhythm;
Of rain hitting the cabin roof.
Provides the beat that is needed;
And this here poem is the proof.

The creek isn't the only thing filling up;
Grass is not the only surface that is wet.
The ink is overflowing like the river;
A flood of words is a safe bet.

Just like the rain providing nourishment;
For the grass, trees and flower.
It also feeds the poets need;
Growing words by the hour.

REALITY SHOW

Some say the most beautiful place on Earth;
Has to be the Garden of Eden.
But they have never spent any time;
On my farm on an April evening.

I just saw a Hen cross the field;
As a Hawk soared 20 feet over head.
Three Deer sneaking through the woods;
As the Sun goes down, headed for their bed.

I saw three Hens this morning;
And a Tom strutting and fanned out.
This is the most beautiful place on Earth;
To me there is no doubt.

An Amish buggy just went down the road;
Something you don't see in the city.
This entertainment goes to waste everyday;
It seem like such a pity.

But I have the best seat in the house;
Here on the front porch of the cabin.
I can't wait until tomorrow night;
To see what else will happen.

Spend some time in the country;
If you are ever able.
I can guarantee this reality show;
Beats the hell out of cable.

HYPELESS HUNTER

They say you can't kill a Buck;
Without a thousand dollar bow.
You gotta have food plots;
To make their antlers grow.

You need a range finder;
To know what pin to use.
You have to do the research;
On what broadheads to choose.

I've got fixed blades from Rural King;
A fifteen-year-old, 3rd owner bow.
Arrows right out of the box from Walmart;
That you think are too heavy and slow.

In the last seven hunts;
I've arrowed five deer.
Three Does and a button buck;
An 8-pointer wider than his ears.

Two forty yard shots;
One at thirty and two at twenty.
Feet per second, I haven't a clue;
But accuracy and punch I have plenty.

SHITTY FOOD

I just walked out the cabin door;
Man did my nose get a whiff.
Somebody has been working the fields;
Because the air smells like shit.

Manure has been spread generously;
Not just the kind of little white lies;
This is the real deal;
The kind that burns your eyes.

I can't believe people would put shit on their food;
That is basically what they are doing.
It ain't coming out of their butts;
But on the farm field you are pooing.

That's why I don't eat that crap;
There is no pun intended.
I ain't no tree hugger;
But even I am offended.

I will stick to the big three;
Beef, Deer and Turkey.
I like real tasty meat;
It will be by proxy if I eat a dingle berry.

SICKLE BAR

I found a new place to hang out;
Didn't have to dress up or go to town.
It's open 24 hours a day, everyday;
No waiting in line to get another round.

There ain't no vying for a waitress' attention;
Never heard the words "Last call".
No sign of a hot bartender;
But hey, you can't have it all.

Not much of a crowd shows up;
Unless my friends happen to stop by.
You always got one in the well;
And the tap never runs dry.

So come on down and join me;
It's really not that far.
Front porch drinkin' at it's finest;
Hanging out at the Sickle Bar.

ONE LAST BUZZ

I went to take a drink;
And said, "What the hell?".
A wasp splashing in my glass;
Like he fell into a well.

Thought maybe I should save him;
Decided to let him drown.
It's not like that Son-of-a-Bitch;
Was going to buy me a round.

Waited until he was pickled;
Then flicked him through the air.
I guess he learned his lesson;
Drink with me if you dare.

Don't waste my good vodka;
If you take it drink it all.
One thing I can say;
Wasps can't handle their alcohol.

He wasn't much of a stinger;
That he once was.
His bark worse than his bite;
But he had one hell of a buzz.

HAPPY TEARS

Walking across the bean stubble;
Among the tracks of turkey and deer.
Moisture on the ground, but not from the rain;
It's from my falling tears.

Celebrating a decade of pleasure;
Of owning this piece of ground.
A blessing most people don't have;
Only those who do would understand.

I've spent a lot of money and time;
To be able to call it my place.
And as long as I get to keep it;
There will be a smile on my face.

Some day I'll return it to God;
Because he is letting me use it.
He knows it is in good hands;
And that I'll never abuse it.

I don't know when my lease is up;
When He'll come collect it, or how many years.
I'll keep it as long as He allows me;
Until I run out of these happy tears.

BLESSES AND SUCCESSES

Sometimes these hunting trips;
Don't turn out the way I planned.
But the failures make me a better hunter;
The week of solitude, a better man.

It's not just about harvesting game;
At least by my standards it shouldn't be.
Time to reflect on life and relationships;
Work on things between God and me.

Thank him for all of his blessings;
Everything for me he has done.
Both the struggles and tribulations;
The love in the past and the love to come.

Success can be measured;
In a multitude of ways.
No sightings or shots fired;
Sometimes were my best hunting days.

It gave me time to think;
And to see things clear.
When I get my life in line;
He blesses me with a turkey or deer.

BUILDING BLISS

Some days I almost feel guilty;
Keeping all this peace to my own.
Four days alone all to myself;
No T.V., no internet and phone.

Sitting here in total solitude;
Sometimes it almost seems.
You could actually see the seasons change;
And watch the trees and field turn green.

Did you know it sometimes takes hours;
For a cloud to move across the sky.
And sometimes you can be so happy;
All you can do is sit and cry.

For almost a full decade;
I have worked for a moment like this.
I dreamt about it and built it;
It has been nothing but bliss.

The only voices I've heard down here;
Are those coming through the radio.
Nothing but real country music;
The beat soft and slow.

Tom T Hall, Skeeter and Don Williams;
Jim Reeves, Hank, Conway and Loretta Lynn.
Soon I'll have to return to reality;
But first chance I get, I'll do it again.

SEARCHING FOR SERVICE

An hour into my hunting trip;
My phone went on the blink.
I wasn't going to miss it;
Or so I didn't think.

But suddenly I began to realize;
I was truly on my own.
Irrelevant to the rest of the world;
Never thought I'd miss a dial tone.

No Facebook, Instagram or texting;
No ability to make or receive a call.
I could take pictures or videos;
But no way to share them all.

How did I get so dependent;
On this hand held device.
I would create a survey;
But have no followers to ask advice.

So I went totally old school;
And grabbed my paper and pen.
I'll just share my thoughts with myself;
Until I can get a hold of Verizon.

WAITING ON TOMORROW

There is not much going on here;
On this April Sunday afternoon.
I'm just sitting on the cabin porch;
Watching the bottles of sun tea brew.

The truck has been unloaded;
Sheets and blankets on my bed.
Hunting camp has been established;
Visions of gobbling Toms in my head.

Waiting on the sun to go down;
Though I don't wish the time away.
But I'm anxious for the morning;
Because tomorrow is my opening day.

I love these warm temperatures;
And all of the sounds of Spring.
The woods are coming alive again;
Fields and trees are turning green.

All I can do now is wait;
For tomorrow and the sun to come up.
Because I will be in the woods;
Safely tucked in my camo pop up.

For now I'll just enjoy the quit time;
Sitting here all alone.
Tomorrow I'll worry about the hunting;
And hopefully bring a big Tom home.

LISTENING TO LEGENDS

Hanging out on the cabin porch;
With Willie, Haggard and Cash.
Before I get to my death date;
I'm working on extending that dash.

Not doing much of anything;
Except avoiding the everyday hassle.
But I'll saddle up pretty soon;
And meet Marty in El Paso.

Wynette is standing by us;
Even though Jones and I are hittin' the white lightning'.
Killing time with Clint;
Was never so excitin'.

Getting baptized by the Kentucky rain;
Dolly says it beats working 9 to 5.
Tennessee Ernie says owing the company store;
Ain't no way to spend your life.

Six day on the road with Dudley;
Is about all I can handle.
All my rowdy friends are coming over tonight;
Including that crazy Rockin' Randall.

FREEDOM RINGS

Nothing makes you appreciate freedom;
Like the National Anthem at noon.
Playing on the local radio station;
Between the classic country tunes.

Watching the stars and stripes flutter;
Shining in the high noon sun.
Makes you eternally grateful;
For what all our Veterans have done.

Because of their brave actions;
I can sit here safely in the middle of my farm.
Protected by those who sacrificed;
To keep us free from harm.

Although I am all alone here;
I stood silently, hat held over my heart.
To honor and respect them;
It's only right to do my part.

So Thank You! To all of you;
You are always welcome to stop by;
And sit with me on the cabin porch;
Drink a beer and watch Ole Glory fly.

OUR CABIN

Ever since I purchased this farm;
I've dreamed about building a cabin.
As the years wore on, the dream remained;
I decided this year to make it happen.

With help from friends and family;
Things have worked out as planned.
Now stands a quaint little cabin;
Surrounded by 40 acres of land.

Built with blood, sweet and tears;
It shines like a diamond in the rough.
I owe it all to the many that helped;
A simple thank you would never be enough.

So to those who found the time;
Who helped me build a Hunting Shack.
You are all welcome to visit anytime;
And I hope you all can come back.

The cabin is always there for you;
It's use is not just for me.
Even if I can't be there;
I'll gladly give you the keys.

It's the least that I can do;
For all the work that you put in.
It may be in the middle of my farm;
But it will always be our cabin.

There is nothing quite as exciting, as taking that final turn and heading onto the dirt road into the property.

The trees are lined up like parade attendees, the dirt starts kicking up form the truck tires like a wind storm is blowing in and God slams a solitude screen door behind you, leaving the outside world on it's own.

One of the hardest to convince that buying the farm was a good investment, was my Father 'J-Pops'. Yet he became the biggest supporter once he visited the property.

It was a big move for me, not only financially, but it meant I would be leaving my huntin' buddies,

'J-Pops', my Brother 'Broadhead', Nephew 'Jake the Snake' and family friend 'Ed-O' who all got me into the game of deer hunting.

'J-Pops' helped my tremendously in the early stages while building the cabin. But the biggest challenge for us was our turkey hunting adventures.

Years before we built the cabin, I introduced him to turkey hunting, so we spent a lot of time down at the farm over a 12 year period. He was never able to kill one at my place, but was successful on a couple of other farms nearby, that he had permission to hunt.

There were some challenging times for both of us, I'm sure. However, there were great times that far out did the challenges.

In 2018, I noticed a big change in Dad, and I thought it was going to be the last season together, because of his physical problems. It was just too hard on him anymore.

So I made sure to do all I could to make it the best year we would have. I took lots of pictures, even had him pose for a couple, like a real shoot. We had deeper conversations than ever and much needed Father and Son time.

Pops did make it down for a few days in the 2019 season, but he was miserable physically and mostly stayed on the porch of the cabin.

Two months later, he passed away. But one of the last things we talked about while he was in the hospital, was how much fun we had at the farm over the years. He grew to absolutely love the place, the hunts, the cookouts, riding the 4-wheeler, the whole experience.

AT LEAST ONE NIGHT

I sit in the glow of the lanterns light;
Protected by walls you helped me build.
One of the first tasks we performed;
To help my dream become fulfilled.

But there is still a missing piece;
Something to complete before it's right.
This dream will not be fully realized;
Until you've stayed here at least one night.

There are others that deserve that honor;
However you should be the first one.
Because without your love and support;
This project would never have begun.

You taught me a long time ago;
Never to give up on my dream.
And here I sit writing in my cabin;
Surrounded by walls of sage green.

It ain't the Taj Mahal;
Nor a big fancy home.
But it is a damn good place;
To sit and pen some poems.

As much as I enjoy it;
Having a safe haven to write.
This story won't be complete;
Until you've stayed here at least one night.

FINAL WALK

I remember the look on his face;
When I mentioned my plan to my Dad.
That I was going to spend some money;
On the 40 acre hunting pad.

He really wasn't sure;
That I had thought this through.
He said, it's you money;
Do what you want to do.

He couldn't envision my dream;
But once he visited the ground.
I could tell he was getting it;
And starting to come around.

When I said I was building a cabin;
He looked at me like I was crazy as hell.
But he came down to hold the stud walls;
As I drove the nails.

He's rode the 4-wheeler there;
And hunted a few days.
Walked every inch of that ground;
Slept in the cabin a few stays.

But this year none of those things mattered;
It was all about time together to talk.
Relive almost 13 years of memories;
As we take perhaps, that final walk.

It's time to fold up the blind;
Put away the old shotgun.
From now on it's about sitting on the porch;
And watching the setting sun.

HUNTING WITH GRANDAD

As I go through preparations;
For another deer hunting season.
This my twenty-sixth year;
But this one is different for one reason.

I never got the privilege;
Of hunting with my Grandad.
In 1976 he made a decision;
That turned out really bad.

Two years ago my Father came over;
And said, "Here is a gift, Son".
A 1925 Winchester 16ga;
Possibly my Grandfather's first gun.

It's been in my Uncle's closet;
All of these lost years.
As I held it in my hands;
I could barely hold back the tears.

Counting down the hours until time;
To don the orange and strap in the stand.
Come opening day you'll find me;
With a piece of Grandad in my hand.

I know one thing is certain;
When I shoulder that gun.
After I fire and that deer buckles;
Lord, the tears are going to come.

The photo album is full of harvested deer;
I've got several heads on the wall.
But this deer is going to be;
The most special of them all.

Without a doubt, the 2018 Deer Season was the most emotional hunt in my entire hunting life. Going into it, I couldn't have scripted the hunt and had it turnout any better than it did.

I was determined to hunt with my Grandfather's (possibly his first gun) 1925 Winchester 16ga shotgun.

I never got to hunt with him growing up. He committed suicide when I was 12 years old.

Not only did I hunt with his gun, I killed an 8-point buck with it and got the kill on video. I have harvested probably 30 or so deer in my 26 years of hunting, including two 150" plus 10-pointers, several 130" plus 8-pointers, but none of them comes close to meaning as much to me as 'Grandpa's Buck' .

To some, this next poem and picture may stir some emotions or make them think and reminisce about their own special hunting spot.

But for me it goes way deeper than that. This picture is the first picture of me on the farm, taken by my Father, on our first visit to walk the property in early 2006. It was an old stand we came across that my neighbor Paul 'Shoot First' Tannahill actually hunted out of when he was younger.

If the image and the poem weren't enough to choke me up. The back story of it and the memories that have followed that day will definitely do it.

My Father was the human version of this stand. Trusty, loyal, familiar, comforting and ultimately aged, worn down by time and so tough to walk away from after our last hunt we had together.

STANDING THE TEST OF TIME

Every hunter has their favorite spots;
Their preferred stand, blind or tree.
There was a time many years ago;
When that go to, sure kill seat was me.

Now that technology has taken over;
Stands are lighter and more portable.
Because the "Pros" wouldn't endorse it;
I have become forgotten, ignored and despicable.

But I remember the time you killed your first deer;
With your Grandpa leaning against my tree.
And the morning of your first solo hunt;
The only one to see it happen, was me.

That long pause before you climbed down;
The last time you hunted from my perch.
Watching you walk away for the last time;
You've no idea how much that hurt.

But I stand here weathered and frail;
After years of inattention and neglect.
In hopes that you would return;
If not to hunt, to show your respect.

Printed in the United States
By Bookmasters